THE CADWALADR QUESTS

The supporting vocabulary revision notebook
for the best-selling **11+** vocabulary novel.

Includes bonus 1000 word 11+ vocabulary list!

THE CADWALADR QUESTS

1

TANGLED TIME
VOCABULARY REVISION NOTEBOOK

EDUCATION BOUTIQUE
A BESPOKE TUTORING SOLUTION

BROOKE MCCLURE · S.L. AGER · LUCY SPENCER

This is a work of fiction. Names, characters, places and incidents either are the product of the author's imagination or are used fictitiously. Any resemblance to actual persons, living or dead, events or locales is entirely coincidental.

The Cadwaladr Quests books have no affiliation with CEM, Durham University, GL Assessment, any school or examination boards.

This book does not purport to be a dictionary, nor does it aim to replace one.

Reading this book does not guarantee your child will pass any exam, but I hope it will help to make learning vocabulary more enjoyable.

Cover design and interior formatting: Mark Thomas / Coverness.com

ISBN 978-1-9993018-5-9

www.slager.co.uk

Table of Contents

Preface

When studying vocabulary for the 11+ and SATs tests at school, my children made lots of notes, often scribbled down onto scattered sheets of lined A4 paper. We eventually made our own vocabulary revision notebook, which we still have. Writing out a word along with its synonyms and antonyms and subsequent sentence application was a key driver in consolidating their learning. Grasping vocabulary takes time, and if possible, it is best started early. I aimed *The Cadwaladr Quests: Tangled Time Vocabulary Novel* at Year 4, 5 and 6 readers, but learning and recording simpler words can begin at any time. In my experience, vocabulary is often the key to comprehension, regardless of the subject, and will also enhance verbal reasoning and creative writing skills. All the best with your learning and have fun scribbling away in your notebook!

Sheena

How to Use This Notebook

We aim to keep notation and revision simple. Below is an example for you to follow. Learn words from the novel *The Cadwaladr Quests: Tangled Time* or fill in the blanks with your own choices. Make your notes then revise until you are a vocabulary expert.

Any word mastered is a **boon**[1].

Example Word

The following example is taken from *The Cadwaladr Quests: Tangled Time:*

Word:	**babble**
Word type:	**verb**
Definition:	**talk rapidly and continuously.**
Synonyms:	**blather, jabber, prattle, gabble, gibber, chatter.**
Antonyms:	**enunciate, articulate, pronounce.**
My sentence:	**I could not grasp what she said because she was babbling and waving her arms ecstatically.**

1 **boon** *(n)* a timely thing that is beneficial or useful; advantage, blessing, windfall, godsend. *(ant)* disadvantage.

My Vocabulary Revision Examples

Word: ____________________

Word type: ____________________

Definition: ____________________

Synonyms: ____________________

Antonyms: ____________________

My sentence: ____________________

Word: ____________________

Word type: ____________________

Definition: ____________________

Synonyms: ____________________

Antonyms: ____________________

My sentence: ____________________

Word:

Word type:

Definition:

Synonyms:

Antonyms:

My sentence:

Word:

Word type:

Definition:

Synonyms:

Antonyms:

My sentence:

Word:

Word type:

Definition:

Synonyms:

Antonyms:

My sentence:

Word:

Word type:

Definition:

Synonyms:

Antonyms:

My sentence:

Word:

Word type:

Definition:

Synonyms:

Antonyms:

My sentence:

Word:

Word type:

Definition:

Synonyms:

Antonyms:

My sentence:

Word:

Word type:

Definition:

Synonyms:

Antonyms:

My sentence:

Word:

Word type:

Definition:

Synonyms:

Antonyms:

My sentence:

Word:

Word type:

Definition:

Synonyms:

Antonyms:

My sentence:

Word: ____________________

Word type: ____________________

Definition: ____________________

Synonyms: ____________________

Antonyms: ____________________

My sentence: ____________________

Word: ____________________

Word type: ____________________

Definition: ____________________

Synonyms: ____________________

Antonyms: ____________________

My sentence: ____________________

Word: ____________________

Word type: ____________________

Definition: ____________________

Synonyms: ____________________

Antonyms: ____________________

My sentence: ____________________

Word:

Word type:

Definition:

Synonyms:

Antonyms:

My sentence:

Word:

Word type:

Definition:

Synonyms:

Antonyms:

My sentence:

Word:

Word type:

Definition:

Synonyms:

Antonyms:

My sentence:

Word:

Word type:

Definition:

Synonyms:

Antonyms:

My sentence:

Word:

Word type:

Definition:

Synonyms:

Antonyms:

My sentence:

Word:

Word type:

Definition:

Synonyms:

Antonyms:

My sentence:

Word:

Word type:

Definition:

Synonyms:

Antonyms:

My sentence:

Word:

Word type:

Definition:

Synonyms:

Antonyms:

My sentence:

Word:

Word type:

Definition:

Synonyms:

Antonyms:

My sentence:

Word:

Word type:

Definition:

Synonyms:

Antonyms:

My sentence:

Word:

Word type:

Definition:

Synonyms:

Antonyms:

My sentence:

Word:

Word type:

Definition:

Synonyms:

Antonyms:

My sentence:

Word:

Word type:

Definition:

Synonyms:

Antonyms:

My sentence:

Word:

Word type:

Definition:

Synonyms:

Antonyms:

My sentence:

Word:

Word type:

Definition:

Synonyms:

Antonyms:

My sentence:

Word: ______________________________

Word type: ______________________________

Definition: ______________________________

Synonyms: ______________________________

Antonyms: ______________________________

My sentence: ______________________________

____

Word: ______________________________

Word type: ______________________________

Definition: ______________________________

Synonyms: ______________________________

Antonyms: ______________________________

My sentence: ______________________________

____

Word: ______________________________

Word type: ______________________________

Definition: ______________________________

Synonyms: ______________________________

Antonyms: ______________________________

My sentence: ______________________________

____

Word:

Word type:

Definition:

Synonyms:

Antonyms:

My sentence:

Word:

Word type:

Definition:

Synonyms:

Antonyms:

My sentence:

Word:

Word type:

Definition:

Synonyms:

Antonyms:

My sentence:

Word: ______________________________

Word type: ______________________________

Definition: ______________________________

Synonyms: ______________________________

Antonyms: ______________________________

My sentence: ______________________________

____

Word: ______________________________

Word type: ______________________________

Definition: ______________________________

Synonyms: ______________________________

Antonyms: ______________________________

My sentence: ______________________________

____

Word: ______________________________

Word type: ______________________________

Definition: ______________________________

Synonyms: ______________________________

Antonyms: ______________________________

My sentence: ______________________________

____

Word:

Word type:

Definition:

Synonyms:

Antonyms:

My sentence:

Word:

Word type:

Definition:

Synonyms:

Antonyms:

My sentence:

Word:

Word type:

Definition:

Synonyms:

Antonyms:

My sentence:

Word: ______________________

Word type: ______________________

Definition: ______________________

Synonyms: ______________________

Antonyms: ______________________

My sentence: ______________________

____

Word: ______________________

Word type: ______________________

Definition: ______________________

Synonyms: ______________________

Antonyms: ______________________

My sentence: ______________________

____

Word: ______________________

Word type: ______________________

Definition: ______________________

Synonyms: ______________________

Antonyms: ______________________

My sentence: ______________________

____

Word:

Word type:

Definition:

Synonyms:

Antonyms:

My sentence:

Word:

Word type:

Definition:

Synonyms:

Antonyms:

My sentence:

Word:

Word type:

Definition:

Synonyms:

Antonyms:

My sentence:

Word:

Word type:

Definition:

Synonyms:

Antonyms:

My sentence:

Word:

Word type:

Definition:

Synonyms:

Antonyms:

My sentence:

Word:

Word type:

Definition:

Synonyms:

Antonyms:

My sentence:

Word: ____________________

Word type: ____________________

Definition: ____________________

Synonyms: ____________________

Antonyms: ____________________

My sentence: ____________________

____

Word: ____________________

Word type: ____________________

Definition: ____________________

Synonyms: ____________________

Antonyms: ____________________

My sentence: ____________________

____

Word: ____________________

Word type: ____________________

Definition: ____________________

Synonyms: ____________________

Antonyms: ____________________

My sentence: ____________________

____

Word: ______________________________

Word type: ______________________________

Definition: ______________________________

Synonyms: ______________________________

Antonyms: ______________________________

My sentence: ______________________________

____

Word: ______________________________

Word type: ______________________________

Definition: ______________________________

Synonyms: ______________________________

Antonyms: ______________________________

My sentence: ______________________________

____

Word: ______________________________

Word type: ______________________________

Definition: ______________________________

Synonyms: ______________________________

Antonyms: ______________________________

My sentence: ______________________________

____

Word:

Word type:

Definition:

Synonyms:

Antonyms:

My sentence:

Word:

Word type:

Definition:

Synonyms:

Antonyms:

My sentence:

Word:

Word type:

Definition:

Synonyms:

Antonyms:

My sentence:

Word:

Word type:

Definition:

Synonyms:

Antonyms:

My sentence:

Word:

Word type:

Definition:

Synonyms:

Antonyms:

My sentence:

Word:

Word type:

Definition:

Synonyms:

Antonyms:

My sentence:

Word:

Word type:

Definition:

Synonyms:

Antonyms:

My sentence:

Word:

Word type:

Definition:

Synonyms:

Antonyms:

My sentence:

Word:

Word type:

Definition:

Synonyms:

Antonyms:

My sentence:

Word: ____________________

Word type: ____________________

Definition: ____________________

Synonyms: ____________________

Antonyms: ____________________

My sentence: ____________________

____

Word: ____________________

Word type: ____________________

Definition: ____________________

Synonyms: ____________________

Antonyms: ____________________

My sentence: ____________________

____

Word: ____________________

Word type: ____________________

Definition: ____________________

Synonyms: ____________________

Antonyms: ____________________

My sentence: ____________________

____

Word: ____________________

Word type: ____________________

Definition: ____________________

Synonyms: ____________________

Antonyms: ____________________

My sentence: ____________________

Word: ____________________

Word type: ____________________

Definition: ____________________

Synonyms: ____________________

Antonyms: ____________________

My sentence: ____________________

Word: ____________________

Word type: ____________________

Definition: ____________________

Synonyms: ____________________

Antonyms: ____________________

My sentence: ____________________

Word:

Word type:

Definition:

Synonyms:

Antonyms:

My sentence:

Word:

Word type:

Definition:

Synonyms:

Antonyms:

My sentence:

Word:

Word type:

Definition:

Synonyms:

Antonyms:

My sentence:

Word:

Word type:

Definition:

Synonyms:

Antonyms:

My sentence:

Word:

Word type:

Definition:

Synonyms:

Antonyms:

My sentence:

Word:

Word type:

Definition:

Synonyms:

Antonyms:

My sentence:

Word: ____________________

Word type: ____________________

Definition: ____________________

Synonyms: ____________________

Antonyms: ____________________

My sentence: ____________________

____

Word: ____________________

Word type: ____________________

Definition: ____________________

Synonyms: ____________________

Antonyms: ____________________

My sentence: ____________________

____

Word: ____________________

Word type: ____________________

Definition: ____________________

Synonyms: ____________________

Antonyms: ____________________

My sentence: ____________________

____

Word:

Word type:

Definition:

Synonyms:

Antonyms:

My sentence:

Word:

Word type:

Definition:

Synonyms:

Antonyms:

My sentence:

Word:

Word type:

Definition:

Synonyms:

Antonyms:

My sentence:

Word:

Word type:

Definition:

Synonyms:

Antonyms:

My sentence:

Word:

Word type:

Definition:

Synonyms:

Antonyms:

My sentence:

Word:

Word type:

Definition:

Synonyms:

Antonyms:

My sentence:

Word: ______________________________

Word type: ______________________________

Definition: ______________________________

Synonyms: ______________________________

Antonyms: ______________________________

My sentence: ______________________________

____

Word: ______________________________

Word type: ______________________________

Definition: ______________________________

Synonyms: ______________________________

Antonyms: ______________________________

My sentence: ______________________________

____

Word: ______________________________

Word type: ______________________________

Definition: ______________________________

Synonyms: ______________________________

Antonyms: ______________________________

My sentence: ______________________________

____

Word:

Word type:

Definition:

Synonyms:

Antonyms:

My sentence:

Word:

Word type:

Definition:

Synonyms:

Antonyms:

My sentence:

Word:

Word type:

Definition:

Synonyms:

Antonyms:

My sentence:

Word:

Word type:

Definition:

Synonyms:

Antonyms:

My sentence:

Word:

Word type:

Definition:

Synonyms:

Antonyms:

My sentence:

Word:

Word type:

Definition:

Synonyms:

Antonyms:

My sentence:

Word:

Word type:

Definition:

Synonyms:

Antonyms:

My sentence:

Word:

Word type:

Definition:

Synonyms:

Antonyms:

My sentence:

Word:

Word type:

Definition:

Synonyms:

Antonyms:

My sentence:

Word:

Word type:

Definition:

Synonyms:

Antonyms:

My sentence:

Word:

Word type:

Definition:

Synonyms:

Antonyms:

My sentence:

Word:

Word type:

Definition:

Synonyms:

Antonyms:

My sentence:

Word:

Word type:

Definition:

Synonyms:

Antonyms:

My sentence:

Word:

Word type:

Definition:

Synonyms:

Antonyms:

My sentence:

Word:

Word type:

Definition:

Synonyms:

Antonyms:

My sentence:

Word:

Word type:

Definition:

Synonyms:

Antonyms:

My sentence:

Word:

Word type:

Definition:

Synonyms:

Antonyms:

My sentence:

Word:

Word type:

Definition:

Synonyms:

Antonyms:

My sentence:

Word: ____________________

Word type: ____________________

Definition: ____________________

Synonyms: ____________________

Antonyms: ____________________

My sentence: ____________________

____

Word: ____________________

Word type: ____________________

Definition: ____________________

Synonyms: ____________________

Antonyms: ____________________

My sentence: ____________________

____

Word: ____________________

Word type: ____________________

Definition: ____________________

Synonyms: ____________________

Antonyms: ____________________

My sentence: ____________________

____

Word:

Word type:

Definition:

Synonyms:

Antonyms:

My sentence:

Word:

Word type:

Definition:

Synonyms:

Antonyms:

My sentence:

Word:

Word type:

Definition:

Synonyms:

Antonyms:

My sentence:

Word: ______________________________

Word type: ______________________________

Definition: ______________________________

Synonyms: ______________________________

Antonyms: ______________________________

My sentence: ______________________________

____

Word: ______________________________

Word type: ______________________________

Definition: ______________________________

Synonyms: ______________________________

Antonyms: ______________________________

My sentence: ______________________________

____

Word: ______________________________

Word type: ______________________________

Definition: ______________________________

Synonyms: ______________________________

Antonyms: ______________________________

My sentence: ______________________________

____

Word:

Word type:

Definition:

Synonyms:

Antonyms:

My sentence:

Word:

Word type:

Definition:

Synonyms:

Antonyms:

My sentence:

Word:

Word type:

Definition:

Synonyms:

Antonyms:

My sentence:

Word: ______________________________

Word type: ______________________________

Definition: ______________________________

Synonyms: ______________________________

Antonyms: ______________________________

My sentence: ______________________________

____

Word: ______________________________

Word type: ______________________________

Definition: ______________________________

Synonyms: ______________________________

Antonyms: ______________________________

My sentence: ______________________________

____

Word: ______________________________

Word type: ______________________________

Definition: ______________________________

Synonyms: ______________________________

Antonyms: ______________________________

My sentence: ______________________________

____

Word:

Word type:

Definition:

Synonyms:

Antonyms:

My sentence:

Word:

Word type:

Definition:

Synonyms:

Antonyms:

My sentence:

Word:

Word type:

Definition:

Synonyms:

Antonyms:

My sentence:

Word:

Word type:

Definition:

Synonyms:

Antonyms:

My sentence:

Word:

Word type:

Definition:

Synonyms:

Antonyms:

My sentence:

Word:

Word type:

Definition:

Synonyms:

Antonyms:

My sentence:

Word:

Word type:

Definition:

Synonyms:

Antonyms:

My sentence:

Word:

Word type:

Definition:

Synonyms:

Antonyms:

My sentence:

Word:

Word type:

Definition:

Synonyms:

Antonyms:

My sentence:

Word:

Word type:

Definition:

Synonyms:

Antonyms:

My sentence:

Word:

Word type:

Definition:

Synonyms:

Antonyms:

My sentence:

Word:

Word type:

Definition:

Synonyms:

Antonyms:

My sentence:

Word:

Word type:

Definition:

Synonyms:

Antonyms:

My sentence:

Word:

Word type:

Definition:

Synonyms:

Antonyms:

My sentence:

Word:

Word type:

Definition:

Synonyms:

Antonyms:

My sentence:

Word:

Word type:

Definition:

Synonyms:

Antonyms:

My sentence:

Word:

Word type:

Definition:

Synonyms:

Antonyms:

My sentence:

Word:

Word type:

Definition:

Synonyms:

Antonyms:

My sentence:

Word:

Word type:

Definition:

Synonyms:

Antonyms:

My sentence:

Word:

Word type:

Definition:

Synonyms:

Antonyms:

My sentence:

Word:

Word type:

Definition:

Synonyms:

Antonyms:

My sentence:

Word:

Word type:

Definition:

Synonyms:

Antonyms:

My sentence:

Word:

Word type:

Definition:

Synonyms:

Antonyms:

My sentence:

Word:

Word type:

Definition:

Synonyms:

Antonyms:

My sentence:

Word:

Word type:

Definition:

Synonyms:

Antonyms:

My sentence:

Word:

Word type:

Definition:

Synonyms:

Antonyms:

My sentence:

Word:

Word type:

Definition:

Synonyms:

Antonyms:

My sentence:

Word:

Word type:

Definition:

Synonyms:

Antonyms:

My sentence:

Word:

Word type:

Definition:

Synonyms:

Antonyms:

My sentence:

Word:

Word type:

Definition:

Synonyms:

Antonyms:

My sentence:

Word:

Word type:

Definition:

Synonyms:

Antonyms:

My sentence:

Word:

Word type:

Definition:

Synonyms:

Antonyms:

My sentence:

Word:

Word type:

Definition:

Synonyms:

Antonyms:

My sentence:

Word:

Word type:

Definition:

Synonyms:

Antonyms:

My sentence:

Word:

Word type:

Definition:

Synonyms:

Antonyms:

My sentence:

Word:

Word type:

Definition:

Synonyms:

Antonyms:

My sentence:

Word:

Word type:

Definition:

Synonyms:

Antonyms:

My sentence:

Word:

Word type:

Definition:

Synonyms:

Antonyms:

My sentence:

Word:

Word type:

Definition:

Synonyms:

Antonyms:

My sentence:

Word:

Word type:

Definition:

Synonyms:

Antonyms:

My sentence:

Word:

Word type:

Definition:

Synonyms:

Antonyms:

My sentence:

Word:

Word type:

Definition:

Synonyms:

Antonyms:

My sentence:

Word:

Word type:

Definition:

Synonyms:

Antonyms:

My sentence:

Word:

Word type:

Definition:

Synonyms:

Antonyms:

My sentence:

Word:

Word type:

Definition:

Synonyms:

Antonyms:

My sentence:

Word: ____________________

Word type: ____________________

Definition: ____________________

Synonyms: ____________________

Antonyms: ____________________

My sentence: ____________________

Word: ____________________

Word type: ____________________

Definition: ____________________

Synonyms: ____________________

Antonyms: ____________________

My sentence: ____________________

Word: ____________________

Word type: ____________________

Definition: ____________________

Synonyms: ____________________

Antonyms: ____________________

My sentence: ____________________

Word:

Word type:

Definition:

Synonyms:

Antonyms:

My sentence:

Word:

Word type:

Definition:

Synonyms:

Antonyms:

My sentence:

Word:

Word type:

Definition:

Synonyms:

Antonyms:

My sentence:

Word: ____________________

Word type: ____________________

Definition: ____________________

Synonyms: ____________________

Antonyms: ____________________

My sentence: ____________________

Word: ____________________

Word type: ____________________

Definition: ____________________

Synonyms: ____________________

Antonyms: ____________________

My sentence: ____________________

Word: ____________________

Word type: ____________________

Definition: ____________________

Synonyms: ____________________

Antonyms: ____________________

My sentence: ____________________

Bonus 11+ Vocabulary List

abashed
abbreviate
abhorrent
absolute
abundance
abysmal
accompany
accomplice
accomplished
accurate
acquire
address
adept
adhere
adjacent
admonish
adolescent
adorn
adversity
advocate
aeon
affable
affectionate
affluent
agile
agitation
ailing

aisle
akin
alcove
alibi
allay
allure
ally
amateur
ambition
amenable
amiable
amid
analyse
anecdote
animosity
antique
antiquity
anxiety
apex
apparent
apparently
apparition
applause
applicant
apprehension
apt
ardent

arduous
aroma
arouse
array
arrogant
artefact
artful
ascend
ashen
askew
aspiration
assess
assiduous
astute
asunder
atrocious
attentive
attire
attribute
audacious
audible
austere
authentic
avert
avid
avow
awry

baffle
bait
baleful
barbaric
barely
bargain
barren
barricade
beckon
bedraggle
behest
beige
belligerent
bellow
bemused
benefit
benevolent
berate
beseech
besiege
bestow
betrayal
beverage
bewilder
bitter
bleak
bleary

blithely
blossom
bludgeon
blurt
bogus
boisterous
bough
brandish
brash
breach
brittle
broach
brooding
buckle
bumbling
burden
burrow
bustling
calf
callous
camouflage
candidate
capacious
captor
career
cascade
catastrophic

cavernous
cease
chagrin
chaos
chaotic
chaperone
charlatan
cheeky
cherish
chide
chief
chisel
chortle
churn
civil
clad
clamber
clarify
clemency
coarse
coincidence
commence
committed
community
companion
compassion
compel
complement
complicit
compliment
comply
compose
comprehend
comrade
concede

conceit
concise
condemn
confer
confess
confidence
confident
congest
conquer
conscience
conscientious
consciousness
consent
consider
conspire
constant
contemplate
contempt
contest
contract
contraption
contrition
convenient
converge
coo
core
corroborate
costly
counsel
countenance
courteous
covert
covet
cower
coy

crafty
crave
craven
credible
crestfallen
crevice
crimson
crockery
crude
cultivate
curiosity
curly
custom
customary
cynical
dab
daub
dazzling
debate
debilitate
debrief
deceive
decline
decoy
deed
defeat
deflate
degrade
dejected
deliberate
delve
demise
dense
depict
depreciate

descendant
despicable
despise
despite
despondent
destination
destiny
deteriorate
detest
detour
detrimental
detritus
devious
devise
devote
devour
dignity
dilapidated
diligently
din
dingy
diplomacy
diplomatic
dire
disarray
discern
disconcert
discreet
disembark
dishevelled
dismal
disperse
dispute
disrupt
distort

dither
divert
dominant
don
dormant
dour
drench
dub
dubious
dupe
dutiful
duty
duvet
dwelling
dwindle
earnest
eclipse
eerie
elated
elegant
eloquent
elude
elusive
embellish
emerge
emit
empathy
employ
employment
enclose
encounter
endeavour
enigmatic
entire
enviable

envy
equine
eradicate
erase
errand
erratic
escalate
exacerbate
exasperated
excavate
exertion
expel
expensive
exquisite
extensive
exterior
extinguish
extortionate
extraordinary
extravagant
extrovert
exuberant
facade
faithful
falter
fanatical
fastidious
fate
fatigue
faultless
feline
feminine
feral
ferocious
fervent
fetid
feverish
fiasco
fickle
fitful
flabbergast
flamboyant
flaunt
flawless
fledgling
flee
flourish
flummox
fluorescent
flutter
foe
foil
folk
fond
foreboding
forefront
forewarn
forfeit
forlorn
former
forthcoming
fortuitous
fortune
foul
fragile
frail
frantic
fraught
fretful
frivolous
fund
furious
furore
furtive
futile
gait
gallant
gargantuan
garish
garment
gauge
gawk
glade
glare
gloat
gloomy
glorious
glory
glower
gnarled
grace
graceful
grand
grateful
grave
graze
gregarious
grief
grieve
grimace
grimy
grisly
grotesque
guffaw
gullible
gush
hamper
hapless
harmony
harrowing
haste
haven
haze
hearsay
heartache
hectic
heed
heir
heirloom
hideous
hinder
hitherto
hollow
honour
horde
hospitable
host
hostile
hue
humble
humiliate
hunch
hurtle
idyllic
imminent
impeccable
impending
imperative
imposter
impudent
incandescent
incessant
incompetent
incongruous
inconsolable
inconspicuous
incredulous
indelible
indignant
industrious
inedible
inept
infamous
inferior
infinite
ingenious
inhabitant
inherit
injurious
injustice
innocuous
innovator
inquisitive
insistent
insolent
intact
integrity
intensify
interior
intervene
intolerable
introvert
invaluable
invigorate
irate

isolate
Jealousy
jeer
Jeopardy
jittery
jolt
jostle
jovial
joyous
justice
keen
kin
knead
knowledge
kudos
lair
lament
languid
languish
lark
latter
legacy
leisure
lenient
lethargic
liable
linger
listless
lithe
livid
loath
loathe
loathsome
lofty
lone
longing
loom
loyal
ludicrous
luscious
lustre
luxurious
maestro
majestic
major
malady
malevolent
malice
malicious
manoeuvre
margin
masquerade
meagre
meander
meaningful
medieval
meek
melancholic
melodic
menacing
mercy
mere
merely
merriment
mesmerise
meticulous
mimic
miniature
minimal
minor
minuscule
mirthful
miscellaneous
miscellany
mischievous
miserly
mock
moderate
modest
monotonous
morsel
mortal
mourn
mucky
mull
muse
muster
mutual
myriad
naive
nausea
negotiate
nimble
noble
nonchalant
nourish
novel
oasis
obligation
oblivion
oblivious
obscure
obsessive
obsolete
obstinate
obtain
odious
offend
omen
ominous
onerous
opaque
oppressive
opulence
ordeal
originally
ostentatious
outrage
outstanding
overrule
overwhelm
pact
painstaking
pallid
pallor
paltry
pandemonium
parallel
paralyse
pardon
partial
participant
pasture
peevish
pensive
perceive
perilous
perish
permit
perpetually
perplex
persistent
personal
pertinent
pervasive
petrify
petulant
piercing
pinnacle
piteous
pithy
pity
placid
plausible
pledge
ploy
plume
plummet
plunder
plunge
plush
polite
pompous
ponder
populous
portentous
portly
postpone
potent
pout
practice
practise
precarious
precede
predicament

predictable	quash	repulse	sarcastic	shrill
premonition	quaver	reputation	saunter	shuffle
prestige	queer	reserve	savour	shun
prevail	quell	reside	scant	sibling
priceless	quench	residual	scarce	silhouette
primarily	queue	resign	scarcely	simper
prime	quip	resort	scarlet	sincere
priority	quiver	respite	scatter	sinister
pristine	quizzical	resplendent	scenic	sketch
privilege	quote	restore	scent	skilful
proclaim	racket	retaliate	sceptical	sleek
prodigious	ramble	reticent	scholar	sleuth
profession	ramshackle	reunite	scoff	slick
proffer	rank	reverence	scold	sliver
proficient	raucous	revive	scorch	sly
profit	ravenous	revolting	scorn	smirk
profound	realm	ridicule	scowl	smuggle
profuse	reap	rift	scupper	snigger
progressive	rebellious	rigorous	secluded	snipe
prohibit	recall	riveted	seek	snob
prolong	reckless	robe	seize	snoop
prominent	recuperate	robust	seldom	sober
prompt	refine	rowdy	semblance	sodden
promptly	refrain	rudimentary	sentiment	solace
prosperous	refute	rueful	sentimental	sole
protrude	reign	rumour	sentry	solitary
provoke	relevant	rural	separate	sombre
pummel	relinquish	ruse	serial	sophisticated
punctual	reluctant	ruthless	serpentine	sorrow
pungent	reminisce	sacred	sever	sovereign
puny	remorse	sacrifice	severe	sow
pursue	renegade	salary	sham	sparse
pursuit	repel	sallow	shard	speck
quaint	repent	sanction	sheer	speckle
quarry	repugnant	sarcasm	shrewd	spectator

spellbind
spherical
spiteful
splay
sporadic
sprawl
spurn
squander
squint
squirm
stalk
stark
startling
statuesque
steep
stern
stifle
stocky
stoop
stout
strategy
stray
strenuous
stress
strive
stubborn
stupendous
sturdy
suave
subdued
submissive
subordinate
subside
substantial
subterfuge

subterranean
subtle
suburban
succumb
sufficient
sullied
summit
summon
superficial
superfluous
superior
surpass
surveillance
suspect
suspend
swollen
sympathy
tarmac
taunt
taut
tease
tedious
temperature
tempestuous
tenacious
tenacity
tend
tendril
tentative
tepid
territory
texture
thaw
theatre
thrive

throne
throng
thrum
thrust
thwart
timid
tint
tirade
tiresome
toil
torment
torrent
torso
tournament
toxic
traitor
tranquil
transaction
transient
transparent
traverse
treacherous
treason
treaty
tremor
trifle
trill
triumphant
trivial
tumult
turmoil
twelfth
tyrant
ubiquitous
unambiguous

uncanny
undermine
unfathomable
Unfurl
union
unique
unison
unite
unorthodox
unpredictable
unruly
unveil
unwilling
unwitting
uproar
urban
urge
utensil
vacant
vaguely
vain
valiant
vanquish
vantage
vapour
variety
vast
vehement
venerable
vengeful
venue
veto
vexed
victorious
vigilant

vigorous
vindictive
virtuous
virulent
vivid
vociferous
volatile
vow
vulgar
waft
wan
warren
wary
weary
whim
whimper
whine
wholly
wield
willing
willowy
wilted
wily
wince
wiry
wisdom
wither
withhold
woe
wretched
yacht
yearn
yelp
yield
yonder

Learn With *The Cadwaladr Quests* Series

Your *The Cadwaladr Quests: Book 1 - Tangled Time Vocabulary Revision Notebook* forms part of *The Cadwaladr Quests* integrated education series.

Read Book 1 in the series - the vocabulary novel *Tangled Time* - then consolidate your comprehension, creative writing and vocabulary skills with the *Tangled Time Workbook.*

Finally, further test your knowledge with the *Vocabulary Revision Notebook.*

Improve even further, with the subsequent volumes in the series!

Find all the available *The Cadwaladr Quests Series* books online via your local Amazon store.

The Cadwaladr Quests: Book 1 - Tangled Time

Further learning books:
The Cadwaladr Quests: Book 1 - Tangled Time - Workbook
The Cadwaladr Quests: Book 1 - Tangled Time - Vocabulary Revision Notebook

The Cadwaladr Quests: Book 2 - Race For The Gold

Further learning books:
The Cadwaladr Quests: Book 2 - Race For The Gold - Workbook
The Cadwaladr Quests: Book 2 - Race For The Gold - Vocabulary Revision Notebook

Reviews, Please!

If you've enjoyed *The Cadwaladr Quests: Book 1 - Tangled Time Vocabulary Revision Notebook*, please feel free to leave a review online at the book's Amazon page.

Errata & Information

To report any **errata**[1], please email: **errata@slager.co.uk**
If you would like information about new books in *The Cadwaladr Quests* series, please visit:

SLAGER.CO.UK

You can stay up to date with S.L. Ager, author of *The Cadwaladr Quests* series, on social media:

facebook.com/SLAgerAuthor
instagram.com/SLAgerAuthor
pinterest.com/SLAgerAuthor
twitter.com/SLAgerAuthor

For further information about Education Boutique, please visit:

EDUCATIONBOUTIQUE.CO.UK

---

1 **erratum** *(n)* an error in writing or publishing (plural: *errata*).

Printed in Great Britain
by Amazon

54622975R00047